MW01536178

Bobbie Bubbles

Maud Gridley Budlong, E. Hugh Sherwood

Alpha Editions

This edition published in 2021

ISBN : 9789355341129

Design and Setting By
Alpha Editions
www.alphaedis.com
Email - info@alphaedis.com

As per information held with us this book is in Public Domain.
This book is a reproduction of an important historical work. Alpha Editions
uses the best technology to reproduce historical work in the same manner
it was first published to preserve its original nature. Any marks or number
seen are left intentionally to preserve its true form.

BOBBIE BUBBLES

Bobbie Bubbles was the most wonderful bubble blower that ever lived.

No, his father's name wasn't Bubbles, and bubble blowing wasn't the family trade. Maybe the Smiths got their name because their great-great-great-grandfather's grandfather was a blacksmith, and maybe the Johnsons got their name because once, ages ago, a man named John had a son; but Bobbie Bubbles didn't get his name secondhand from anybody. He got it himself, because he was a famous person. And this is how it happened.

One day Bobbie and Betty and Billy were out in the garden blowing bubbles. They all blew bubbles, big ones and little ones, till evening came and it was almost time for tea. Then Billy said, "I can blow the biggest bubble anybody's blown to-day," and blew a bubble as big as an apple.

"I can blow one bigger than that," said Betty, and blew a bubble as big as a toy balloon.

"I'll blow a bigger one still," said Bobbie, and he blew and blew, and the bubble grew and grew—as big as a pumpkin, as big as the snowball they'd rolled in the yard at Christmas.

Even then the wonderful bubble did not stop, but kept growing bigger and bigger. And still Bobbie blew and blew, and still the shining bubble grew and grew.

Then, wonder of wonders! The great shimmering bubble, floating in the sunlit air and glowing with all the colors of the rainbow, suddenly reached out and took in Bobbie—pipe, arm, and all.

Slowly the bubble rose with the surprised Bobbie and, light as thistledown, floated gently to and fro in the soft summer air just above the garden.

"Dear me!" thought Bobbie, looking down through what seemed like walls of gleaming crystal. "Dear me! That's not our garden where Betty and Billy and I blew soap bubbles. No, that rainbow-colored place looks just like Fairyland in our story books. Really, now," thought he, "have we sailed over into Fairyland?"

Then, just as he was wondering what would happen next, along came a puff of wind, and, whiff! away sailed the bubble with Bobbie in it.

Over the trees they went, up toward the clouds. Bobbie looked down through the bubble and saw his house grow smaller and smaller. Soon the whole village was only a little dark speck.

Honk! Honk! Honk!

"Mercy!" thought Bobbie. "Have they automobiles up here?" He looked around at the smooth sides of his delicate airship, but there was no way to steer it that he could see. Honk! Honk! Honk!

"I can't!" shouted Bobbie. "I'd get out of the way if I could, but—"

"Honk! Honk!" cried the leader   Page 1

By this time he'd managed to wiggle around in the bubble so that he could see what was behind him. It was a flock of geese.

"Honk! Honk!" cried the leader again. He seemed to be dashing straight toward the bubble.

"I'd get out of the way if I could—" began Bobbie once more.

"Certainly, certainly," the goose interrupted rudely, "but there's no occasion. Don't you think we've made this trip often enough not to run into things?"

"But you honked," said Bobbie, as the goose flapped his great wing within a feather's breadth of the bubble.

"Why have a danger signal if you don't use it?" answered the goose, craning his head back over his wing; and in a moment nearly the whole flock had skimmed past and were honking away again, though there was nothing in the sky that Bobbie could see.

"What are they honking at now?" he cried to an old goose, straggling behind.

"That rooster on the weather vane," said the goose. "It'd better look out. It's only two miles off." And he went honking on after the others.

Up soared the bubble, and Bobbie soon saw that the clouds now formed themselves into a long, crooked roadway lined with little houses and barns and windmills. Tiny cows grazed on the fleecy pink clouds, like cows in a meadow of pink and white clover. And, strange to say, what had looked like stars were buttercups—golden buttercups.

Soon Bobbie sailed up close to a funny little farmer who was milking a cow.

"Please, sir," Bobbie called to him "will you tell me what country this is?"

The little farmer turned around in such surprise that his stream of milk followed his glance, and came splashing against the side of the bubble. Bobbie held up his hands, for he was thirsty. But the bubble was like a big glass, with Bobbie on the inside and the milk on the outside—and not a drop came through.

Bobbie held up his hands   Page

"Oh, whizaphats!" said Bobbie in disgust. "We don't put even goldfish in such a mean thing as this. At least we leave a hole in the top to put food in!"

"Eh? What's that? I can't hear you," said the little farmer in a squeaky voice.

"Oh!" said Bobbie. "Oh! I was asking you what country this is."

"The Milky Way," answered the little farmer. "This is where we make cheese and butter for his Beaming Majesty the Moon. I'm Chief Cheese Server," he added proudly.

Majesty! Was that jolly looking man in the moon, who'd winked at him so many times, a king? He didn't act very dignified.

"Must be some relation to Old King Cole," thought Bobbie. But before he had time to ask about this, up jumped the little farmer in such haste he overturned his milking stool, which rolled down perilously near the bubble.

Serving his Majesty, the Moon   Page 18

"Time to serve his Majesty!" he cried, and dashed into the house for his court costume. A second later he appeared wearing a wig and goatee like Uncle Sam's and carrying a big cheese on a gold plate. Behind him came a pretty little milkmaid with a glass of buttermilk.

"Follow us," the farmer called out to Bobbie, and the bubble bounced along after them.

"Follow us," the farmer called

They didn't seem to have time to wait for Bobbie, and when he reached the door of the great hall he saw the moon beaming down on them as they stood before his throne. Bobbie wondered what he ought to do when he got in, but just then the bubble was caught up by the wind again, and sailed gently on.

"Well, it's all very queer," said Bobbie. "Anyway, I found out that's all wrong about the moon's being green cheese."

[Ill 9023]

Now just about this time it chanced that the King of Mars picked up his powerful spyglass and began to scan the heavens for signs of possible war. He was a crusty old fellow, the King of Mars, and nothing delighted him so much as to stir up trouble. In fact, he was one of those people who to make things unpleasant, *half* the time they don't mean to. Even in his own court, where he *always* manage when at least wished to appear very nice to every one, his wife was always having to step on his toes—under his royal robes, of course—to remind him to be polite. She'd stepped on them so often, indeed, that he had to have one foot bound up in a bandage.

Now when the king looked out, everything seemed very peaceful and uninteresting. There were the golden buttercups and the fleecy meadows of the Milky Way, and the calm blue sea of the sky—all quiet and everyday looking.

But at length, as he looked at the sky, the king saw a little shining ball sailing up into the air. What could it be? A new planet, perhaps. He sent post haste for charts and maps, but not a thing could he find about any such fairylike world. He was about to declare himself the discoverer of a new heavenly body and to summon his army to conquer its people when another glance through his glasses showed him that this little globe had only one inhabitant, and that one a little boy!

However, no telling but even this little boy might be a spy from some distant land and dangerous, so he summoned his soldiers and ordered them to capture the stranger.

Bobbie surrounded by hundreds of winged men

Away went the soldiers at double quick, and in a moment Bobbie was surrounded by hundreds of little winged men. They had large heads and queer faces; but fortunately, when they saw Bobbie and his frail little "world" they thought it a huge joke and quite forgot to look warlike. They seized the bubble, however, and soon Bobbie was hovering over a great building that reminded him of pictures of either the English House of Parliament or the New York Terminal, he couldn't remember which. Anyway, it was very large and very high.

The king was greatly disappointed to see what a little world he'd found, but nevertheless, he commanded Bobbie to come forth and swear allegiance to him.

Now Bobbie would have been very glad, indeed, to step out of the bubble if he could have gone home, but he didn't much like the looks of the King of Mars. Anyway, as you know, it was quite impossible for him to leave the bubble.

"I can't get out, your Majesty," he said; "and besides, I'm not allowed to swear, so it wouldn't be any use to get out for that."

"Indeed!" cried the king in a great rage. "Indeed! Haven't I conquered your whole world and brought you here prisoner?"

"Why, no," answered Bobbie, frightened to see the king so very angry. "You haven't conquered my world at all. You don't think this little bubble is a world, do you? It's nothing but soap and water and air—a fairy balloon, my mother says—though why it's grown so big and sailed off with me like this, I'm sure I don't; know."

"Oh, it's water, is it? Well, then, why don't you say flowing? Say flowing, not sailing. Water doesn't sail, it flows," cried the king. "Your language is something terrible. The whole thing's a case for the naval authorities. Admiral, scuttle this water balloon so the prisoner cannot flow away, and put the enemy under guard. But mind you don't wreck the water balloon. We'll use it as a model for our new fleet." Poor little Bobbie! He had stuck a pin in a soap bubble one day, and he remembered how suddenly it collapsed into a little spot of soapy water. If they scuttled his bubble now, how would he ever get home?

The king's funny little special guard was rushing forward with his spear to pierce the bubble, and Bobbie was almost ready to cry, when he heard a tinkling voice, and looking up he saw the daintiest of little fairies standing before the king. Without a doubt she was queen of the fairies. Bobbie seemed to know her quite well, he had seen her picture often in his picture books at home.

Bobbie was almost ready to cry

"Your Majesty," she was saying, "this little boy is no enemy of yours. His mother was quite right; what you thought was his world is indeed a fairy balloon, and though he didn't know it, he is on his way to Flowerland at the special wish of the fairies. Will you not let him go?"

"Will you not let him go?"

Now the King of Mars well knew the power of the fairies, and he usually listened to what they said; but it made him so angry to think he'd made such a mistake as to believe the fairy balloon a new world he shouted, "No! I'll not let him go! Put him under guard. Put 'em both under guard—put—" But before he could say another word, with a great buzzing and whirring, a whole host of fairy soldiers had fallen upon him. They stabbed the poor king right and left with their sharp little sabers and bayonets, so that he shrieked with pain and rage and—quite forgetting his bandaged foot—rushed down from his throne toward the door of the palace. Then the fairy soldiers fell upon the king's funny little admiral, and all the king's men, and drove them off helter skelter. The soldiers followed swiftly after them, and when they rushed past Bobbie, to his surprise he saw they were a swarm of bees!

He rushed down from his throne

At the same time the bubble began to rise. As it floated through the window Bobbie could see the king and his men tearing madly round and round the palace yard. My! how angry they were, and how their arms and legs did smart where the soldiers had stabbed them!

They stabbed the poor king right and left with their sharp little sabers and bayonets, so that he shrieked with pain and rage and—quite forgetting his bandaged foot—rushed down from his throne toward the door of the palace. Then the fairy soldiers fell upon the king's funny little admiral, and all the king's men, and drove them off helter skelter. The soldiers followed swiftly after them, and when they rushed past Bobbie, to his surprise he saw they were a swarm of bees!

At the same time the bubble began to rise. As it floated through the window Bobbie could see the king and his men tearing madly round and round the palace yard. My! how angry they were, and how their arms and legs did smart where the soldiers had stabbed them!

The fairy summoned her soldiers, and the next instant they were all sailing away.

To Flowerland the wee fairy took Bobbie, and here were sights to gladden one's heart. As far as he could see, spread great beds of brilliant tulips and nodding columbine, towering flowers that Bobbie could not name, and delicate trailing vines. Bees and butterflies half hidden in the blossoms made fluttering bits of brightness. Beautiful dragon flies darted about, and Bobbie could hear the soft whir of the humming birds' wings, though all he could see of them was a gold-green flash as they darted from flower to flower. The air was sweet with perfume, and as Bobbie gazed about there suddenly burst through the blossoms a band of smiling fairies.

A band of smiling fairies burst through the blossoms

There were seven of them, dressed in the seven colors of the rainbow, and as the dew-drops fell from the flowers upon their wings they sparkled like diamonds in the sunlight.

Half flying, half dancing, they circled Bobbie

Half flying, half dancing, they circled round Bobbie and his fairy and led them to a tiny bower overhung with vines. In the center stood a great toadstool that served as a table, and around it smaller toadstool chairs. Upon the table was spread a wondrous banquet. There was honey in dainty flower cups, and the most delicious-looking food that Bobbie had ever seen. Gay-winged butterflies with lily-pad trays and little butler bees in smart striped waistcoats hovered about to serve the banquet.

As Bobbie and the queen approached the table, five other fairies came tripping into the bower. "These are my faithful helpers, Bobbie," said the queen, "my Right-hand Fairies. Thumb, how went the day?"

"Most happily, your Majesty," answered a little fairy in a tight-fitting suit, and as he spoke he made a quick bow backwards, for all the world like a thumb straightening up stiffly.

"And yours, Pointer?" asked the queen.

"The same, your Majesty," answered the fairy next to Thumb, and as she spoke she made a most curious bow with her whole body bent over from the ankles, so that she looked like a finger pointing straight and stern.

"And Middleman?" asked the fairy queen, addressing the tallest of the five.

"Most excellently, your Majesty," replied Middleman. He was so tall and dignified he scarcely bowed at all.

"Circlet next," said the queen, and the fourth little fairy made a correct bow from the waist, like a polite gentleman at a ball.

"Delightfully, your Majesty," he said. "And how did your day go, Little One?" said the queen, turning to the smallest of the fairies.

"It was a beautiful day, your Majesty," she replied, and made a little curly looking bow so that her hair touched the floor.

"Ah, then," said the queen, "let us refresh ourselves."

So they all gathered around the table and the bees and butterflies began to serve them—all but Bobbie; for the bubble was still as smooth as glass. He remembered how he had tried to get a drink in the Milky Way, and looked at the queen questioningly. She turned to him.

"You cannot leave your fairy balloon, Bobbie," she said, "unless you will stay with us a hundred years. But you need only wish for whatever you would like to eat, and you will find it in your hand."

Bobbie wished for one delicious thing after another

So Bobbie wished for one delicious thing after another, and each tasted better than the last. As the sun went down, fireflies danced into the bower and lighted it with their tiny candles until the moon spread its soft white light over all the land.

Then, the fairy banquet finished, the queen rose from the table. "Now for a frolic," she said to Bobbie, and as the Right-hand Fairies circled about them she led the way to where all the fairies of Flowerland were dancing on the green. Bobbie, of course, could not dance, shut up in the bubble, but Bobbie wished for one delicious thing after another he was so interested in watching the fairies' graceful, fantastic figures and mischievous pranks, he never thought of dancing himself; and when at cockcrow the fairies suddenly slipped out of sight in the flowers, he could scarcely believe it was day.

Back to the bower floated the bubble, and Bobbie slept until the sun was high in the morning sky. Then the fairy queen called him, and he awoke to see the Rainbow Fairies just outside. They were seated on brilliant butterflies which were harnessed to a spiderweb net.

"To-day you shall visit the Rainbow," said the queen.

"And see the pot of gold?" asked Bobbie.

"Yes," answered the fairy, "and all the countless treasures the Rainbow Dwarf guards there."

[Ill 945]

Then the Rainbow Fairies slipped down from the butterflies and threw the silken strands of the spiderweb net over the bubble.

The fairy queen mounted her own golden butterfly, and away they flew.

Away they flew

They hadn't gone very far when they met the four little Breezes frolicking in the air. They bobbed their heads up and down three times out of respect to the fairy queen, but all the time they were looking out of the corners of their eyes at Bobbie.

"These are the Breezes, Bobbie," said the fairy, "the sons of the four Winds," and turning to them, she added, "But perhaps you know Bobbie?"

Bobbie was sure he had never seen the Breezes before, but they seemed to know him.

"Oh, can't he stay and play with us?" cried West Breeze. But at that moment a big dirigible came in sight, and the four little Breezes went scurrying away.

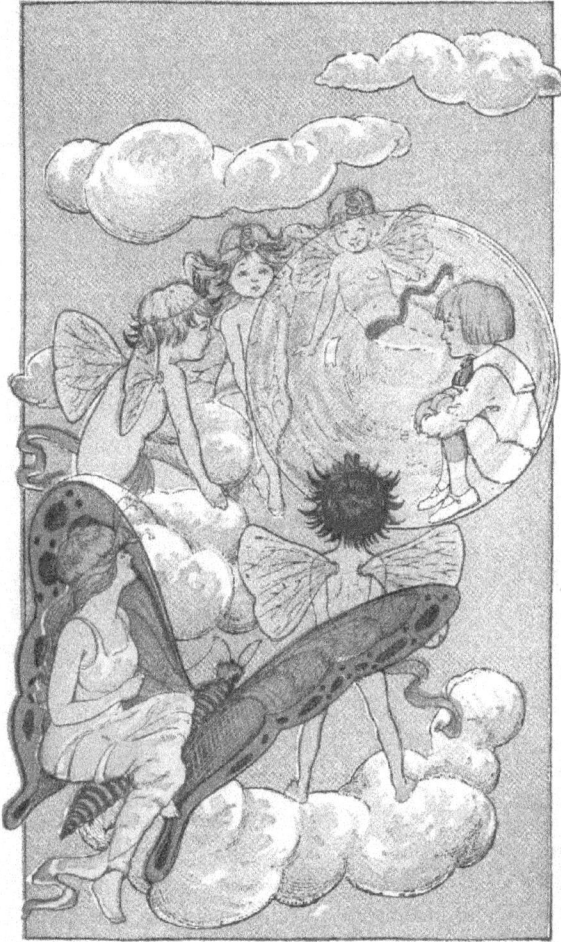

Bobbie was sure he had never seen the Breezes before Page 42

In it were four strange looking persons. Bobbie thought they must be sky pirates until the fairy introduced them as the four Winds! He wondered how such dreadful looking fathers could have such nice little sons.

"Bobbie has been my guest since yesterday, and we 're now on our way to the Rainbow," explained the fairy.

"We are on our way to the Rainbow, too," said North Wind, and his breath was so chilly the butterfly steeds huddled together in fright.

"Let us take Bobbie with us, your Majesty," said West Wind, and gave Bobbie a tremendous, friendly wink. "He ought to have a ride in our new dirigible—it's great!"

Bobbie did wish he could have gone with the little Breezes instead of with their fathers, but he did n't like to offend West Wind, so he said, "I'd be glad to go with you, but I'd rather ride in my own balloon, please."

"Very well," said the fairy. "That will be delightful, and I'll leave you. Have a good time!" and with that she waved good-by and flew back toward Flowerland with her butterfly team.

The bubble floated alongside the dirigible, though the four Winds made such a gale with their constant talk and laughter the bubble certainly would have been blown to pieces if it had n't been a fairy balloon instead of an ordinary bubble. As they went along the brothers began planning what they would do to entertain Bobbie after they left the Rainbow.

"We'll go down to Earth," said West Wind. "That's the place to have fun! I'll blow off a man's hat and make him chase it, and I'll flap some washing off a line and let a dog get it, and—"

"And I 'll blow up a rain," interrupted East Wind, "and turn an umbrella wrong side out, and upset a signboard and a sailboat, and—"

"What child's play!" said North Wind freezingly. "You must come with me, Bobbie. I'll show you a polar bear riding on an iceberg, and then we'll blow the berg crashing down on an ocean liner, and—"

"Have a good time" Page 45

Bobbie began to be frightened. He didn't think he'd enjoy doing any such thing. He was wishing he'd never come with the Winds when he heard a great commotion behind him, and *their* father, old King Eolus himself, came puffing up.

"Here, you young scalawags," he shouted in a big voice, "what's all this nonsense? Where are you going? I know where you are going—you 're going home, straight home."

"Sorry, sir," said West Wind impudently, "but we told the fairy queen we'd take her friend Bobbie to the Rainbow."

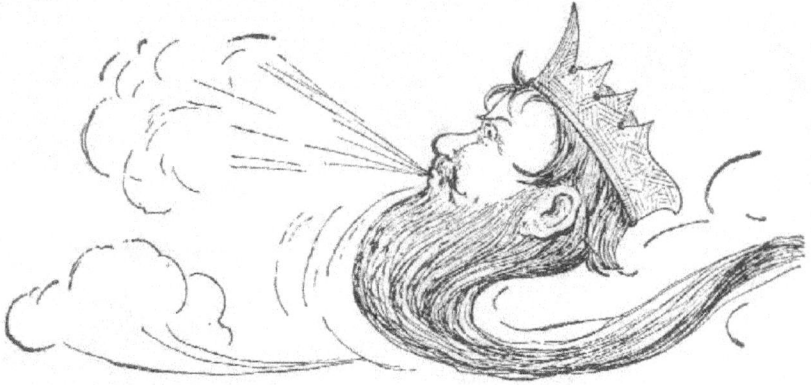

"I'll take him there myself," said the old king. "That's just what I'm here for." So the four Winds had to say good-by to Bobbie and go back home; and Bobbie wasn't sorry to see them go, either.

"My messengers, the geese, told me yesterday that you were up here," said the old king. "I've been on the lookout for you ever since. I was afraid you'd fall in with those rascals of mine. They 're good boys," he added, not stopping to think he'd just called them rascals, "good boys, but young."

"Oh," said Bobbie.

Then old King Eolus and Bobbie traveled on together until they came to a great shimmering many-colored arch. At the foot of the arch stood the Rainbow Dwarf beside the pot of gold, and piled around him were bags of coins and jewels, chests of silver, and wonderful jars and horns of precious metal. Their splendor dazzled one's eyes.

At the foot of the arch stood the Rainbow Dwarf

"All hail!" cried the dwarf.

"Good day!" cried King Eolus. "No hail in this weather."

But the Rainbow Dwarf didn't seem to see that any joke was intended, and was as solemn as an owl.

"Did you see my daughters?" he asked Bobbie, so suddenly poor Bobbie could only gasp for a moment.

"Did you see my daughters in Flower-land?" he questioned again.

"Oh, the Rainbow Fairies," answered Bobbie. "Yes; but why do they live in Flowerland? Why don't they live here with you?"

"Listen to me, son," answered the dwarf solemnly. "Listen to me. My daughters are the artists for all Fairyland. I taught them to paint here in the Rainbow, and now they paint all the flowers and trees and green things that grow. That's why they live in Flowerland. But they often come to visit me, and of course they have to come back to the Rainbow to get their paint."

Just then Bobbie heard the soft fluttering of wings, and looking up he saw coming toward him the seven dainty Rainbow Fairies. With them was the fairy queen seated on her golden butterfly and driving her brilliant butterfly team. Bobbie was very glad to see the beautiful little fairies again, and they all greeted him and the little dwarf affectionately.

Each carried a long dandelion stem with a fuzzy head

But the fairies seemed in a great hurry. Each carried a long dandelion stem with a fuzzy white head. One by one they went up to the rainbow, dipped the dandelion brush in gleaming color, and, in a second, were off again to Flowerland. The fairy queen told Bobbie of the new violets and buttercups, nodding sunflowers, and fields of new grass waiting to be painted by the Rainbow Fairies. Then she bade Bobbie good-by once more, and waving her hand to the dwarf, mounted her shining steed and flew swiftly away toward the golden sun.

As Bobbie watched her, old King Eolus came puffing back from the chest of silver he'd been examining. "Time for me to be off again," he said. "Old Eolus can't stay in one place very long, you know. Come on, Bobbie, and I'll start you on your way home!"

"Here, here," cried the dwarf, "before you go, help yourself to some of this treasure. It's the prize for reaching the Rainbow's end, and you've done it, Bobbie."

But again Bobbie could not reach through the bubble, and much as he hated to leave the glittering coins and sparkling stones, there seemed no help for it. He was just about to thank the dwarf for his kindness, however, when the dwarf said, "Next time you see the Raindrops, dig in your back yard. They are my messengers, and I'll send the gold by them."

So Bobbie thanked the dwarf for his promise, and bade him good-by. Then old King Eolus puffed out his cheeks and with a mighty breath sent the bubble spinning. Faster and faster it sped through space, and what with going so fast and thinking so hard about the gold the dwarf had promised him, Bobbie never noticed what was happening around him until he heard a hoarse voice shouting, "Off the track! Off the track! Off the track!"

Imagine how shocked he was to see coming toward him a most remarkable person who was all head and no body—though at first glance the long sandy beard that trailed out behind him took the place of a body. But, indeed, he was no gentleman in any sense of the word. He had wicked looking eyes, and as he shouted again he pointed with one of his great ears.

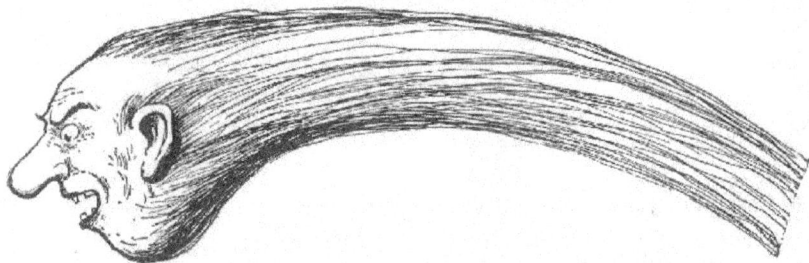

"Off the track! Off the track! Off the track!" he repeated at the top of his voice.

Now Bobbie could n't see any track, and of course he couldn't have got off of his own accord if he had seen one. This curious person was coming like a fire engine, too, and things certainly seemed in a bad way.

"He's just like those silly geese," thought Bobbie. "Folks up here in the sky are always telling other folks to get out of the way!"

Now the air was filled with a terrible rushing sound and the curious person was shouting away louder than ever. "Clear the road, clear the road there for the Comet Express!"

"Whizaphats!" thought Bobbie. "Comet Express! Why, he *can't* stop— expresses never stop—and I can't—and—I'll signal him!"

He grabbed at his red tie and, pulling it off his neck, waved it round and round his head. Too late—the Comet Expressman still dashed madly on.

"Say," cried Bobbie, "don't you see this signal? Danger! Danger, I tell you! There'll be a collision!"

Bobbie grew more and more excited as he watched the grinning head with the long sandy beard rushing on and on. As it neared the Milky Way a flock of goats scurried wildly across its path and a herd of cows kicked up their heels and ran to the farthest corner of their pink pasture. And just then, with a fearful swoop, the Comet Express bore down upon Bobbie and the wonderful bubble.

The Comet Express bore down upon Bobbie   Page 60

Whiz! Buzz! Boom! With a whirl and dash the rushing head came tearing along, then—Zip! Spat!

The bubble was splashing in a burst of water and light. The Comet Expressman looked back with an evil grin, and Bobbie went hurtling down—down—over and over—down—down. There below him was the big, deep sea. Down—down went Bobbie, and you may be sure he had no chance to think of any way to stop himself. Sometimes his head was where his heels ought to be, and sometimes he spun around like a top. And what was worse yet, once in a while, as he whirled about, he caught sight of the Comet Expressman, and that hideous head with the long sandy beard trailing out behind would wiggle its ears and grin.

My! but Bobbie would have given anything to get hold of that long trailing sandy beard and give it a sharp tug or two.

But just holding his breath gave Bobbie enough to do.

Down—down—he fell—over and over—down and down. He caught one more sight of the wiggling ears when—Splash!

But to his surprise Bobbie did n't stop. He kept on going down, down through the soft green water. Away, 'way down he went, to the bottom of the deep sea.

"Well, anyway," thought he, "I'm done with the Comet Expressman."

He could see nothing but water, and more water, and he certainly felt wet clear through. Then, having reached the bottom, Bobbie had another surprise. He began going up again as fast as he had gone down, and in a moment found himself on the surface, being carried swiftly along by a great foaming wave that was rushing toward the sandy shore, and—

Bump!

There sat Bobbie in his garden at home!

No wonder he was wet. The bubble bowl was upset and Fluff, the poodle, was just disappearing behind the lilac bush. The soapy water made a nice, cold, soaky puddle.

A big, round, shining moon that made him think of the Comet Expressman seemed to be looking down and laughing at him.

The garden was very quiet. Looking around, Bobbie spied a little white fuzzy head close beside him.

"Fairy paint brush! Humph!" thought Bobbie, and he reached over to pluck a blade of grass. "Why, I declare," he said, "the little new shoot just peeping out of the ground has almost no color at all. Think of all the grass that's been painted right in our own yard! Those Rainbow Fairies certainly have a good deal of work to do." As Bobbie stood up, Fluff came bounding back. He leaped upon his little master as joyfully as though he had n't seen him for days and weeks. For a minute Bobbie felt that he really had been away on a long, long journey. Then he glanced down at the soapy little puddle behind him.

"Fluff, sir," he said with a frown, pretending to be very angry, "look at what you've done, and look at my clothes! But my whizaphats!" he added, seizing Fluff's paws. "If that dream had been true your ocean would have saved my life. If I'd landed on the *ground* when the Comet Expressman hit me, no telling what *would* have happened!"

Just then the tea bell rang. "Come on, Fluff," Bobbie cried, starting for the house, "come on. We can get a drink of milk here, even if it isn't the Milky Way!"

CPSIA information can be obtained
at www.ICGtesting.com
Printed in the USA
LVHW052354021121
702257LV00007B/922

9 789355 341129